Begin Making Music

A first book of musical experiments for young people

Holmes McDougall Limited Edinburgh

1 Instruments to make

Which instruments do you **bang**?

Which instruments do you **shake**?

Which instruments make a **ringing sound**?

See if you can copy some of these sounds, using your mouth, your voice, your hands, your feet.

3 Talk to each other

A game for two.

Talk to each other—**but not with your voice!**

Take one or two instruments each, and talk to each other with them.

Make the **instruments** talk! Sometimes happy!

Sometimes laughing!

Sometimes serious!

Sometimes sad!

Sometimes asking!

Sometimes answering!

Sometimes cross!

Sometimes excited!

Your instruments could play

      quickly,   slowly,   loudly,   quietly.

They could talk together, or they could listen to each other

Do not use your voice!

4 Susie

Farmer Jones had a cow who loved music. She was called
Susie. Susie made her own music. She sang:

Mooooooooo — Mooooooooo
Moo-moo-moo— Mooooooooo

She sang her tune nearly all day. But when she was
eating she could not sing. She made eating noises instead.
At milking time she heard the milking machine say:

click-clack — shshshshshsh
click-clack — shshshshshsh
click-clack — shshshshshsh

She liked singing with the milking machine.
One day in winter she caught a cold. Then—oh dear!—
She lost her voice! She could not sing! She was so unhappy
she could not give Farmer Jones any milk.

The farmer had a good idea. He tied one bell round her neck,
and two more round her tummy. Susie was very
pleased. Now, when she heard the milking machine say:

click-clack — shshshshshsh
click-clack — shshshshshsh

She swayed from side to side, and her bells rang:

bing-bang-bong
bing-bang-bong

Susie liked her bells so much that she would not let
Farmer Jones take them away, even when her cold was better.

Everyone could hear Susie singing:

      Mooooooooooo — mooooooooooo

      Moo-moo-moo— moo-moo-moo

whilst her bells rang:

      Bing-bang-bong

      Bing-bang-bong

And she gave Farmer Jones a lot of milk!

You will need a tune for Susie to **sing**.

Make the sound of her **eating**.

Make the sound of the **milking machine**.

Make the sound of her **bells**.

What do you think Susie looked like?

Act the story of Susie. Make your own picture of Susie
with scrap cloth or paper—anything.

5 Work in pairs

Copying (a) **with instruments:**
One of you plays a short rhythm. The other has to copy it.

(b) **singing:**
One of you makes up a little tune. The other copies it.

(c) **moving:**
One of you makes some movements with your body. The other copies these movements on the instrument.

Make many different kinds of rhythm, tune and movement.

6 Say·and·play

Say aloud:

Say it four times, quickly, without
stopping.
Clap it while you whisper the words.
Play it on an instrument.
Sing a tune for it.

Here is another rhyme to say-and-play.
Play this game with four people.
Each person takes one line:

1   Rain on the house-top
2   Rain on the tree
3   Rain on the green grass
4   But don't rain on me!

Here is another. Say-and-play this
one in as many ways as you can.

7 Games with names

Four people stand round a glockenspiel or a xylophone.

Take it in turns to say-and-play "My name is .... "

Follow each other quickly, with no stopping. Go round many times.

When you can do this easily change your words to:

"My name is............., my friend´s name is............ "

Follow each other quickly as before.

Make a rhyme up about yourself. Make a tune for it.

8 Rowing on the river

It is a very hot summer day. You are rowing a boat along a river.
It is too hot to row fast, so you are rowing very gently.
The oars are making quiet splashes in the water, and they are
rattling a little in their rowlocks. Your dad is asleep
at the back of the boat. He is snoring. You can hear one or
two birds singing in the trees.

Make up some music to describe this scene.
On your tuned instruments use only notes C D E and G.

9 Row the boat (round in four parts)

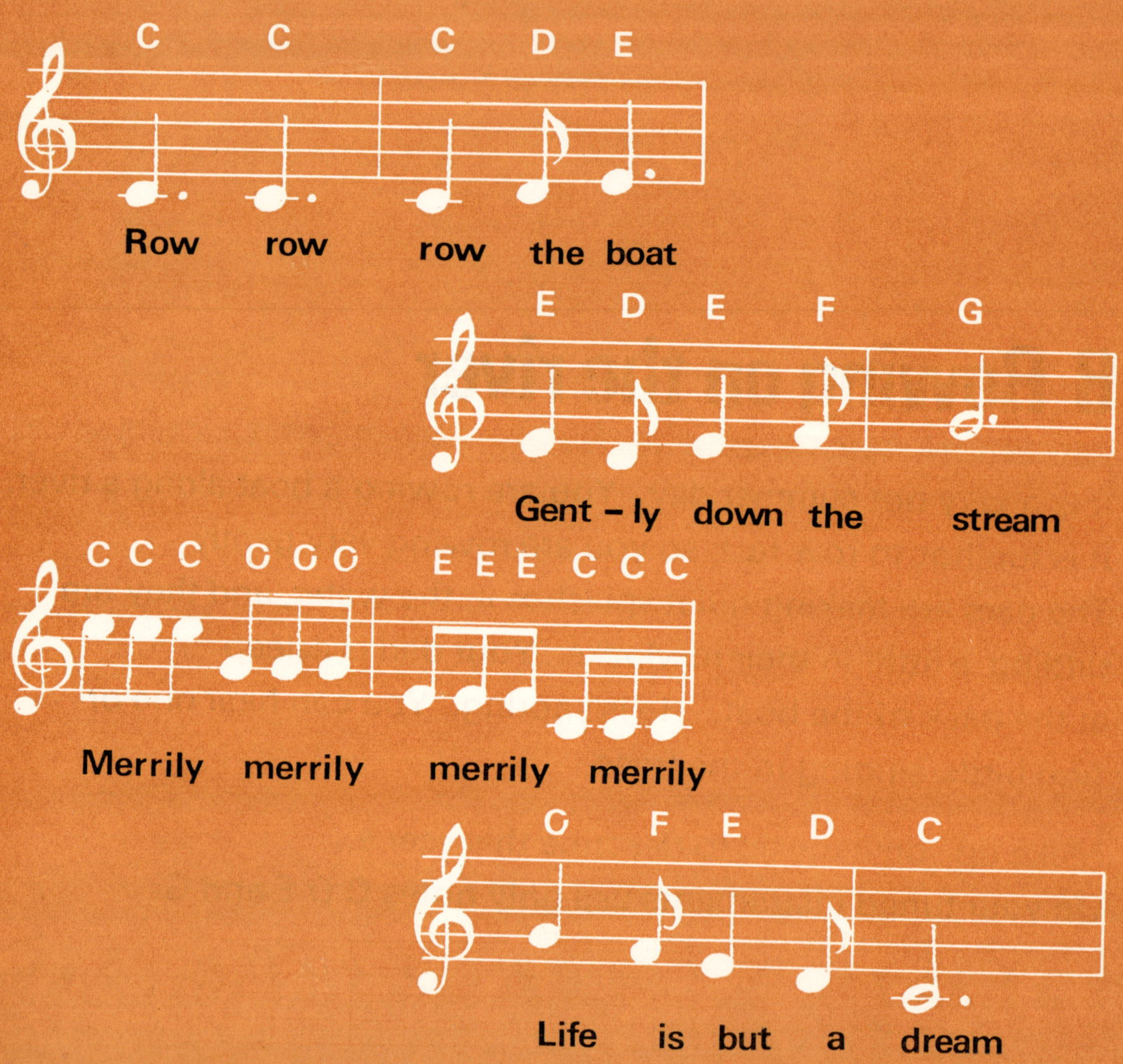

When you can sing this song, make up sounds to go with it.
You can use the sounds that you made for your music
picture "Rowing on the River".

10 Rhymes for singing and playing

When you are making tunes you can repeat words or lines as
much as you like. Do you know a song that goes:

Poor Jenny is a-weeping

a-weeping

a-weeping

Poor Jenny is a-weeping

On a fine Summer's day.

Do you see how the words repeat?
Over the page you will find some more rhymes. Repeat words
in these rhymes if you think it would make a better tune.

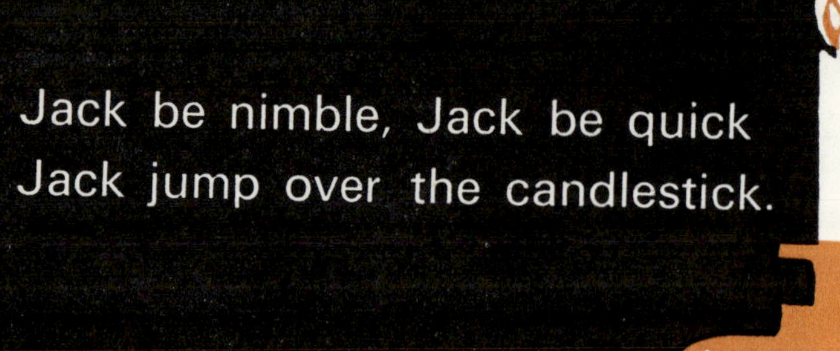

Jack be nimble, Jack be quick
Jack jump over the candlestick.

Jerry Hall
He is so small
A rat could eat him
Head and all.

Turn about, turn about,
Jump, Jim Crow.
Every time I turn about
I do just so.

Shoe the horse and shoe the mare
But let the little colt go bare.

I won't be my father's Jack
I won't be my father's Jill
I will be the fiddler's wife
And I'll have music when I will.
T'other little tune,
T'other little tune,
Prithee love, play me
T'other little tune.

11 A music picture

A monkey is playing in his cage. Sometimes he jumps very
fast; sometimes he sits and eats a nut.

The keeper comes. He is very big, and he has heavy
boots on.

He walks slowly. He stops to open the cage. His keys
rattle as he opens the gate.

The monkey watches. As the gate opens he jumps
down and rushes out.

The keeper runs after him, but the monkey runs up a tree and
laughs.

Pretend you are the monkey, and the keeper.
Do what they do.
Make up music to go with what you do.

12 A sad song

Ned, Ned,
The donkey's dead.
He died last night
With a pain in his head.

Say-and-play it many times.

Find sad sounding instruments.

Find three notes that make a sad tune.
Say-and-play, using the sad sounding notes.
Sing the song as you play.

13 Hallowe'en

Heigh ho! for Hallowe'en,
All the witches to be seen,
Some black and some green,
Heigh ho! for Hallowe'en.

This time choose instruments and notes that sound
frightening. Make a witches' dance.

14 Question and answer songs

Two people can make tunes for these two poems, one sings the question, and the other sings the answer. Add instruments later.

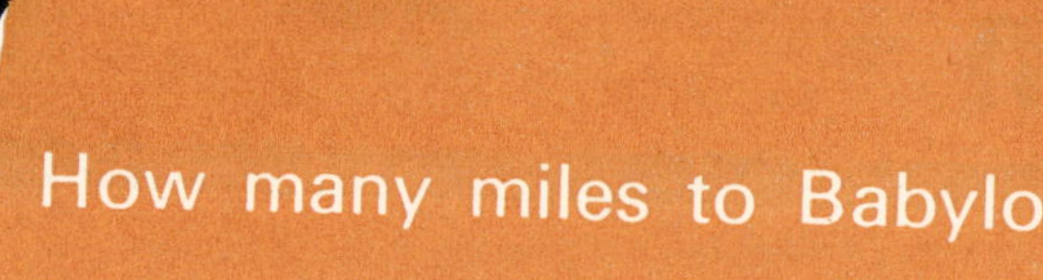

Make your own question and answer rhyme. "Going shopping" "Asking Dad" "Arguing" "What is this?" Make a tune for it.

15 The tailor and the crow

There was once a tailor who was a real crosspatch! He was
thin and bony, and he could always find something to
grouse about (Tailor's music).

One day in summer, as he was sitting under a tree mending
his cloak, he heard a "Caw! Caw!", and there above
him sat a crow, watching him at work (Crow's music).

"Hey, bring me my bow and arrow!" shouted the tailor
to his wife—without even a "please."

The poor woman, who was always frightened of her
husband, ran off to get the bow in a great hurry.
(Make the sound of her footsteps).

Soon she came back (footsteps).
By this time the tailor was so angry—with her and with the
crow—that his hands were shaking as he took aim.
(Tailor's music—try to make it 'shaky').

Now just beyond the tree was a large fat sow with eight
little piglets (music for the sow). The tailor fired his arrow
but—oh dear—it missed the crow and hit the poor old sow
instead. With a moan she sank to the ground
(sow's music).

    "Hey, wife! quick, fetch some brandy", shouted the
tailor. But it was too late. The old sow died, and the
bell tolled sadly (sad music).

Tell the story with your music
Act the story with your music
On the next page there is a song about this story.

16 The carrion crow

A carrion crow sat on an oak,
Hey derry down, derry di-do
Watching a tailor mending his cloak,
Caw, caw, the carrion crow
Hey derry down, derry di-do.

"Oh wife, O wife, bring here my bow"
Hey derry down, derry di-do
"That I may shoot this carrion crow." (refrain)

The tailor he fired, but missed his mark,
Hey derry down, derry di-do
For he shot his old sow right bang through the heart.
(refrain)

"O wife, O wife, bring brandy in a spoon"
Hey derry down, derry di-do
"For our old sow is down in a swoon." (refrain)

The old sow died and the bell did toll
Hey derry down, derry di-do
And the little pigs prayed for the old sow's soul. (refrain)

Make music to go with the song. Use some of the
music you have already made.

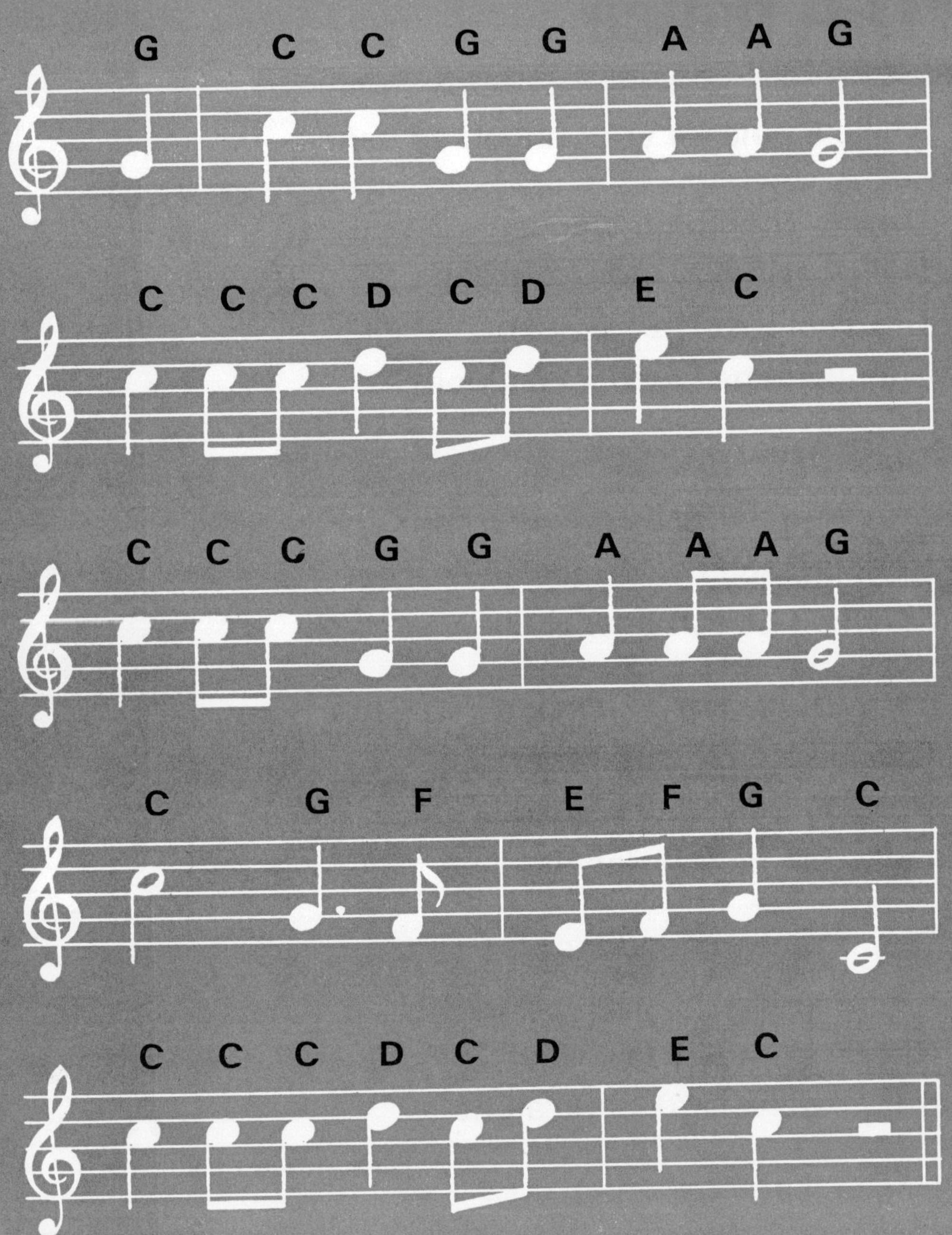

By permission of J. Curwen & Sons Limited,
28 Maiden Lane, London, W.C.2. From "English Folk Songs for Schools."

17 A dance

Make a tune for your fingers to dance.

Dance, Thumbkin, dance.
Dance ye merry men, everyone,
But Thumbkin he can dance alone,
Thumbkin he can dance alone.

Dance, Foreman, dance.
Dance ye merry men everyone,
But Foreman he can dance alone,
Foreman he can dance alone.

Dance, Longman, dance.
Dance ye merry men everyone,
But Longman he can dance alone,
Longman he can dance alone.

Dance, Ringman, dance.
Dance ye merry men everyone,
But Ringman he can dance alone,
Ringman he can dance alone.

Dance, Littleman, dance.
Dance ye merry men everyone,
But Littleman he can dance alone,
Littleman he can dance alone.

18 More rhymes

Diddle diddle dumpling, my son John
Went to bed with his trousers on,
One shoe off and one shoe on,
Diddle diddle dumpling, my son John.

Mother may I go and bathe?

Yes, my darling daughter.

Hang your clothes on yonder tree

But don't go near the water!

(Make another verse for the daughter's answer).

One to make ready,
And two to prepare.
Good luck to the rider,
Away goes the mare.
(Make her gallop away into the distance).

Diddlety diddlety dumpty,
The cat ran up the plum tree.
Half a crown
To fetch her down,
Diddlety diddlety dumpty.

19 Things that move

Make a sound like a washing machine.
Make the sound of a train going along.
Make them start slowly, get quicker, slow down, and stop.
Here is a machine for hammering. Make the sound of it.

20 Sounds we hear

Make the sound of:

A person walking on the pavement.

A child running through leaves.

A lame man walking.

A child skipping along.

A horse trotting.

Water dripping from a tap on to a tin.

21 Sing, play and dance

A cat came fiddling out of a barn
With a pair of bagpipes under his arm.
He could sing nothing but "Fiddle-de-dee,
The mouse has married the bumble bee."
Pipe, cat, dance, mouse,
We'll have a wedding at our good house.

Some of you say "Pipe, cat, dance, mouse, pipe, cat, dance, mouse."
Say it over and over again, whilst other say the rest of the poem.
Say-and-play "Pipe, cat, dance, mouse" whilst the others are saying the poem.
Some of you pretend to be the cat and say over and over again, "Fiddle-de-dee fiddle-de-dee the mouse has married the bumble bee."

Now in three groups
1. Some of you be the cat.
2. Some of you say "Pipe, cat, dance, mouse."
3. Those who are left say the poem.

Make your voices dance!
And why not dance while you sing the poem?

As you say this rhyme, make the sounds on instruments to
suit the words. Finish with a dance.

The cat sat asleep by the side of the fire.
The mistress snored, loud as a pig.
Jack took up his fiddle, by Jenny's desire,
And struck up a bit of a jig.

Four girls can have some
fun making
a tune for this rhyme.

Oh Mother I'll be married
To Mr. Punchinello.
To Mr. Punch,
To Mr. Chin,
To Mr. Nell,
To Mr. Lo,
Mr. Punch, Mr. Chin,
Mr. Nell, Mr. Lo,
To Mr. Punchinello.

23 Make musical patterns

Step patterns

Make a little tune of only four or five notes. Play it on a
glockenspiel or xylophone beginning on note **A**.
Play it many times until you remember its shape.
Play it beginning on **B** instead of **A**.
Then again, beginning on **C**, then on **D** and so on.
Play it again beginning on **A**. Now again, starting one
note lower—on **G**. Then on **F**, then on **E** and so on.

Side by side patterns

Whilst you play your tune beginning on **A**, your friend
plays it with you, beginning on **C**.
You begin on **A** whilst she begins on **D** (or **E** or **F** or **G**).
Decide which side-by-side pattern you like best.

Upside down patterns

Start your tune on **A** again but make it go the opposite
way on your instrument—the same shape but upside down.
With your friend, try playing your tune the right way
up and upside down—both at the same time. Try different
starting notes.

Changing patterns

Play any of the patterns that you liked best.

Play them **slower**.

Play them **quicker**.

Play them with a **different rhythm**.

Play them on a **different instrument**.

Can you think of any other patterns to make with your tune ?

24 The visitor who was not wanted

Young Roger came tapping at Dolly's window,
    Thumpety, thumpety, thump.
He begged for admittance, she answered him "No",
    Glumpety, glumpety, glump.
"My Dolly, my dear, your true love is here"
    Dumpety, dumpety, dump.
"No, no Roger, no, as you come you may go"
    Stumpety, stumpety, stump.

Make up your own tune and your own dance.

25 Some animals

Choose your instruments and make music for:

a frog croaking and jumping,

a mouse squeaking and running,

a flea hopping,

a cow trying to dance,

a cat miaowing and pouncing,

a snake slithering along.

If you use any tuned instruments, use only **C, D, F, G, A.**

Froggie went a·courting

Note to teacher: as the word rhythm of each verse is different, only the outline of the rhythm is given here.

27 The billy goats gruff

A story to tell and act with your own music

Three Billy Goats lived in a field. They were called Gruff.

One was very small and thin, and he had

a squeaky voice. (music)

The second was bigger and stronger. He had small horns

and a deeper voice. (music)

The oldest Billy Goat was very big and fat.

He had long curly horns and a very gruff voice. (music)

One day the smallest goat wanted to cross the bridge to

the next field.

But under the bridge lived a very fierce and ugly troll. (music)

"Who's that crossing my bridge?
Who's that crossing my very own bridge?
Stop or I'll eat you up!
Stop, or I'll eat you every scrap!"

"Please let me free!
I'll get fat you see.
Can't get any thinner,
No good for your dinner!"

"Who's that crossing my bridge?
Who's that crossing my very own bridge?
Stop, or I'll eat you up!
Stop, or I'll eat you, every scrap!"

"Please, please, let me go.
I'm not really fat you know.
Why not wait and try another?
How about my great big brother?"

"Who's that crossing my bridge?
Who's that crossing my very own bridge?
Stop, or I'll eat you up!
Stop, or I'll eat you every scrap!

"How dare you, how dare you!
I know how to scare you!
Come out and I'll fight you,
I'll butt you and bite you!"

FOR THE TEACHER

This book is intended for the use of children aged between about 7 and 9 years.

A glance at the pages will show that it is not a text-book. The material presented is simply intended as a stimulus to the creation of music, and I have deliberately refrained from too detailed instructions as to technique. If the material is found to stimulate other work in school, such as drama, movement, or art, so much the better.

The **Stories with music** lend themselves to several different treatments, some of which may even be more dramatic than musical. It is hoped that drama, movement and music will have a part to play in any treatment, however, and teachers will find that each stimulates the other. Nor need the teacher be surprised if the children develop their ideas through other creative medium. The treatment of the musical ideas will depend very much on the background of the children. Those with plenty of singing experience will be at some advantage, for they will be able spontaneously to sing tunes for the rhymes, and even to sing wordless tunes when the need arises. For instance the words "Bing-bang-bong" in **Susie** could be sung, or played on three chime bars or other ringing instruments, or they could be both sung and played. I would hope that Susie would actually sing—in as cow-like a manner as possible!—whilst the milking machine is making its noises.

The section, **Talk to each other** is an activity that could well take place often, especially if a large space, hall or playground, is available. Absolute freedom is to be encouraged in this, for the aim is to develop sensitive playing of the instruments, and *not* the development of formal rhythm. Indeed it is as an antidote to metred rhythmic work that this activity is most valuable. It could well be extended to include the use of the mouth, hands, and wordless voice. Various uses of this "conversation" idea can well be combined with movement; for instance, one child "talks" to his partner with his instrument, whilst the other "talks" with his body, or both "talk" with both body and instrument. In this way both the music and the movement will be enriched.

The **Music pictures** are intended to be purely instrumental, with no speech. They could well be accompanied by movement, however, and in this case children could work in small groups, and *either* the music *or* the movement should come first. Thereafter each can build on the other.

In both the stories and the music pictures I would not like to insist that the music is anything more than improvisatory, i.e. played or sung, then forgotten. The character of the music, or even the shape of a tune may be reproduced each time, but each teacher must decide to what extent the improvised music should be remembered exactly and repeated. In most cases the children will make it abundantly clear. A great deal will depend upon their experience of improvisation.

In the **Work with rhymes**, however, I would hope that memorable tunes will be forthcoming. Children love to repeat these rhymes again and again, and tunes will almost certainly be repeated also. For children with little musical experience I suggest that only a few notes are used in the early stages—perhaps only two or three—but the choice might well be made by the children. The limiting of notes assists the memory, and helps the children's ears to focus on definite pitch sounds.

The **Songs** can be sung by the teacher, the children, or both. They can very easily be played by children, especially if several children take one phrase each. In each case work on the story should precede the song itself, so that the ideas produced may be used for the accompaniment of the song, and so that the song will be sung with greater relish and understanding. It will be noticed that the songs are very simple, and lend themselves to easier playing. Remove the notes that are not being used.

It is envisaged that creative activity in music will take place in schools just as naturally as other creative activities. In some cases it will be convenient to have music as one of the many different activities going on in a room at the same time; in others there may clearly be a need for a communal activity. For it is important to remember that music in a school has two aspects: (a) individual development of what I like to call "Musical responsibility", i.e. the ability to play an independent part, either alone or within a group, and (b) the fostering of a spirit of "togetherness" by means of communal music making. Thus no teacher should imagine that the creative activities described in this book are intended to replace the more traditional song-singing approach, but rather to complement it. For further ideas in communal, yet creative, music making, the reader is referred to the teacher's book in this series, **Children Make Music.**

Finally I hope that the ideas in this book will be thought of as only a starting point from which teachers will develop their own.